Animals
HIDDEN
in the
OCEAN

Jessica Rusick

PEBBLE
a capstone imprint

Published by Capstone Press, an imprint of Capstone
1710 Roe Crest Drive
North Mankato, Minnesota 56003
capstonepub.com

Library of Congress Cataloging-in-Publication Data
Names: Rusick, Jessica, author.
Title: Animals hidden in the ocean / Jessica Rusick.
Description: North Mankato, Minnesota : Pebble, [2022] | Series: Animals
undercover | Audience: Ages 5-8 | Audience: Grades K-1 |
Summary: "Some ocean creatures are masters of disguise! They use camouflage
and cover to outsmart predators or sneak up on prey. Some ocean animals blend
in with sand, pebbles, and more. Others hide in coral reefs or beneath the ocean
floor. Can you spot the creatures hidden in the ocean?"-- Provided by publisher.
Identifiers: LCCN 2021041457 (print) | LCCN 2021041458 (ebook) |
  ISBN 9781666315400 (hardcover) | ISBN 9781666318166 (paperback) |
  ISBN 9781666315417 (pdf) | ISBN 9781666315431 (kindle edition)
Subjects: LCSH: Marine animals--Juvenile literature. | Camouflage (Biology)--
Juvenile literature.
Classification: LCC QL122.2 .R85 2022 (print) | LCC QL122.2 (ebook) | DDC 591.77-
-dc23
LC record available at https://lccn.loc.gov/2021041457
LC ebook record available at https://lccn.loc.gov/2021041458

Image Credits
iStockphoto: cinoby, 3 (bottom left), 10, deraugenzeuge, 3 (bottom middle), 7,
ifish, 9, lindsay_imagery, 27, Nigel Marsh, 26, 32 (bottom), Wan Yong Chong,
25; Shutterstock: Alex Stemmer, 3 (bottom right), 6, Andrea Izzotti, 18, 32 (top),
Anne Frijling, 13, Damsea, 5, Daniel Lamborn, 3 (top), 24, Ekkapan Poddamrong,
21, Ethan Daniels, 17, John A. Anderson, 15, Luke Suen, 22, Lynn Archer, 16, 31
(bottom), magnusdeepbelow, 11, Matt9122, 28, nickeverett1981, 1, 14, Paulo
Violas, 8, 23, 31 (top), Richard Whitcombe, 29, 30, SaltedLife, 19, Tom Goaz, Cover,
12, 31 (middle), tropicdreams, 20, 32 (middle)

Design Elements
Mighty Media, Inc.

Editorial and Design Credits
Editor: Rebecca Felix, Mighty Media; Designer: Aruna Rangarajan, Mighty Media
Printed and bound in China. 5196

HIDDEN IN THE
OCEAN

Some ocean creatures are masters of disguise! They use camouflage and cover to outsmart predators or sneak up on prey. Some ocean animals blend in with coral reefs or ocean rocks. Others hide under sand. Can you spot the creatures hidden in the ocean?

First, try to spot the animal hidden in the ocean.

WHAT DO YOU THINK IT IS?

Turn the page to reveal the animal and learn more about it.

DID YOU GUESS RIGHT?

This bright fish has three white bands. What is it?

Turn and see!

Clownfish live in sea anemones. Anemones are animals with long tentacles. These tentacles sting other animals. But clownfish are not hurt by the stings.

This fish has a large mouth. What is it?

Turn and see!

IT'S A FROGFISH!

Frogfish use camouflage to hunt. A frogfish blends in with sponges or coral. It quickly opens its mouth as prey swims by. This pulls water and the prey into the fish's mouth.

This long fish looks like a snake. What is it?

Turn and see!

IT'S A MORAY EEL!

Moray eels have long, slippery bodies. They often hide in coral reefs with only their heads visible. The eels have large mouths. These help the eels catch prey.

This tentacled mollusk is related to an octopus. What is it?

Turn and see!

IT'S A CUTTLEFISH!

A cuttlefish is able to change its shape, texture, and color. It can change colors quickly. This helps it attract a mate.

This small fish has pink spots. What is it?

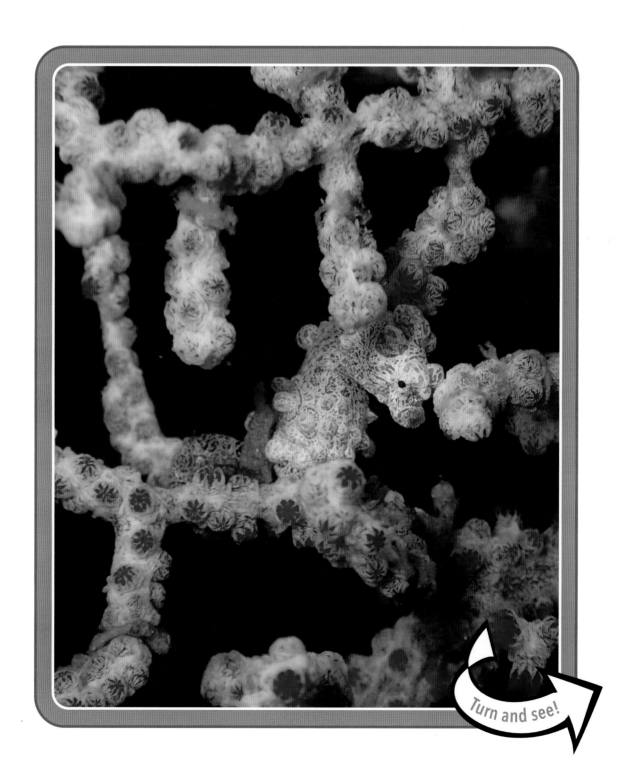

Turn and see!

IT'S A BARGIBANT'S PYGMY SEAHORSE!

Bargibant's pygmy seahorses live in coral. Their bodies look just like the coral. These seahorses are tiny. They are about 0.8 inches (2 centimeters) long.

This spotted fish is flat. What is it?

Turn and see!

IT'S A PEACOCK FLOUNDER!

Peacock flounders can change color. They often blend in with the ocean floor. The fish lie flat in the sand. They catch prey that swims past!

This fish has fringed lips. What is it?

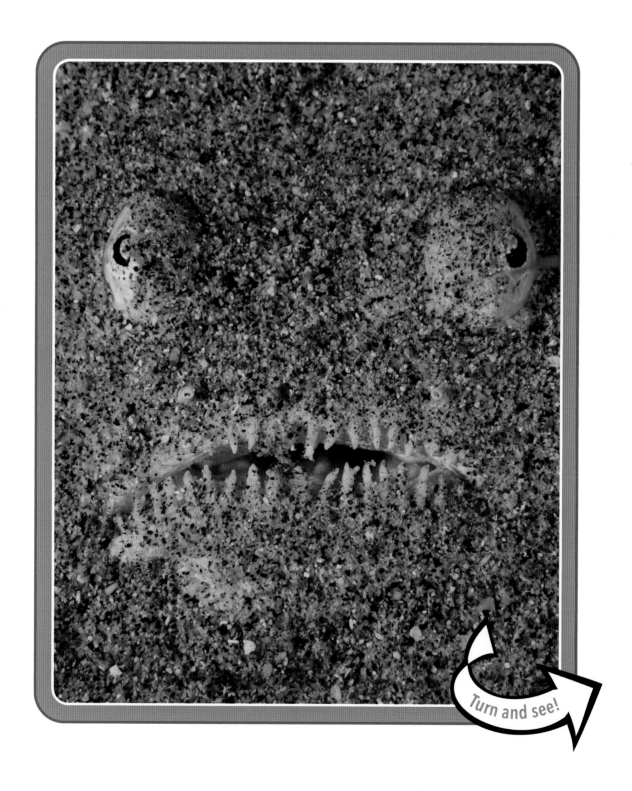

Turn and see!

Stargazers eat small fish and crabs. They bury themselves in sand to hunt. Only their eyes and mouths stick out.

This ocean reptile is a strong swimmer. What is it?

Turn and see!

IT'S A SEA TURTLE!

The shells of most sea turtle species are made of bones and scales. The shell protects the turtle from danger. It also provides camouflage.

This striped swimmer has eight arms. What is it?

Turn and see!

IT'S A MIMIC OCTOPUS!

Mimic octopuses can make themselves look like other animals. One animal is the dangerous sea snake. The octopus waves two of its arms. It hides the rest of its body. This scares away predators!

This rare fish is related to seahorses. What is it?

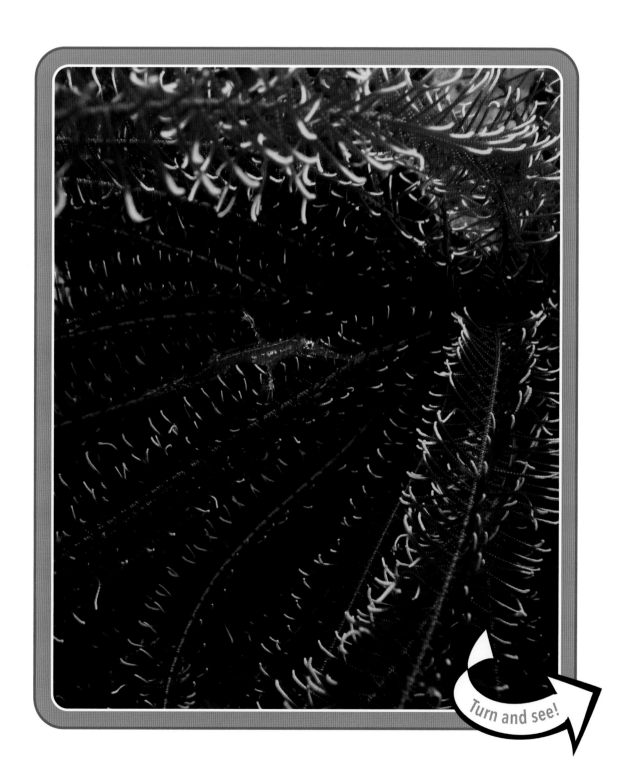

Turn and see!

IT'S AN **ORNATE GHOST PIPEFISH!**

Ornate ghost pipefish have tiny skin flaps. These help the fish hide in coral and sea plants. The fish also have long snouts. They use these to suck up plankton.

This flat fish has long, sharp teeth. What is it?

Turn and see!

IT'S A WOBBEGONG SHARK!

Wobbegong sharks are covered in dark and light spots. They lie on the ocean floor. The sharks open their mouths when prey swims past. The prey gets sucked inside!

This bumpy fish looks like a rock. What is it?

Turn and see!

IT'S A STONEFISH!

Stonefish blend in with rocks and coral. They stay still and wait for prey. Stonefish also have spines on their backs. The spines release venom. This hurts predators!

This finned creature has sharp spines. What is it?

Turn and see!

IT'S A **SCORPIONFISH!**

Scorpionfish hunt at night. The fish sit in rocks or coral reefs. Some have colorful fins that blend in with coral. Others are colored to blend in with ocean rocks. Scorpionfish also use venom to hunt prey.

FUN FACTS

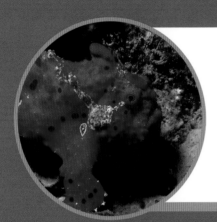

Frogfish use their fins to push them along the ocean floor. This can look like they are walking!

Cuttlefish can see behind them without moving their bodies.

Both of a peacock flounder's eyes are on one side of its head.

Some stargazers can shock prey with electricity.

Sea turtles can weigh up to 2,000 pounds (907 kilograms)!

Wobbegong sharks are also called "carpet sharks." That's because they look like carpets!